Wildebeest

An Amazing Animal Picture Book about Wildebeest for Kids

By

Heather Marshall

Copyright © 2020 by Heather Marshall

All rights reserved

Image Credits: Royalty free images reproduced under license from various stock image repositories. Under a creative commons licenses.

I am a wildebeest.

I am a member of the antelope family.

Some people also call me gnu.

I love to live in green plains and open woodlands.

I have a mane, just like a horse.

I only eat grass.

I move from one place to another to look for food.

I live with my other friends and together we are called a herd.

I am afraid of lions, hyenas and cheetahs.

I have sharp and curved horns.

I have a cow-like face.

I am gray with dark colored stripes.

I am very noisy.

I snort very loudly.

I also moan constantly.

I have a very bushy beard.

When my herd runs, we help new plants to grow.

I love to wake up early in the morning.

At night, we take turns sleeping to keep an eye for our enemies.

We love to run with other animals like the zebras.

I am a fast and agile runner.

I have very powerful hooves.

Made in the USA
Coppell, TX
26 August 2021